Southern African
Development
Community (SAD

MOZAMBIQUE

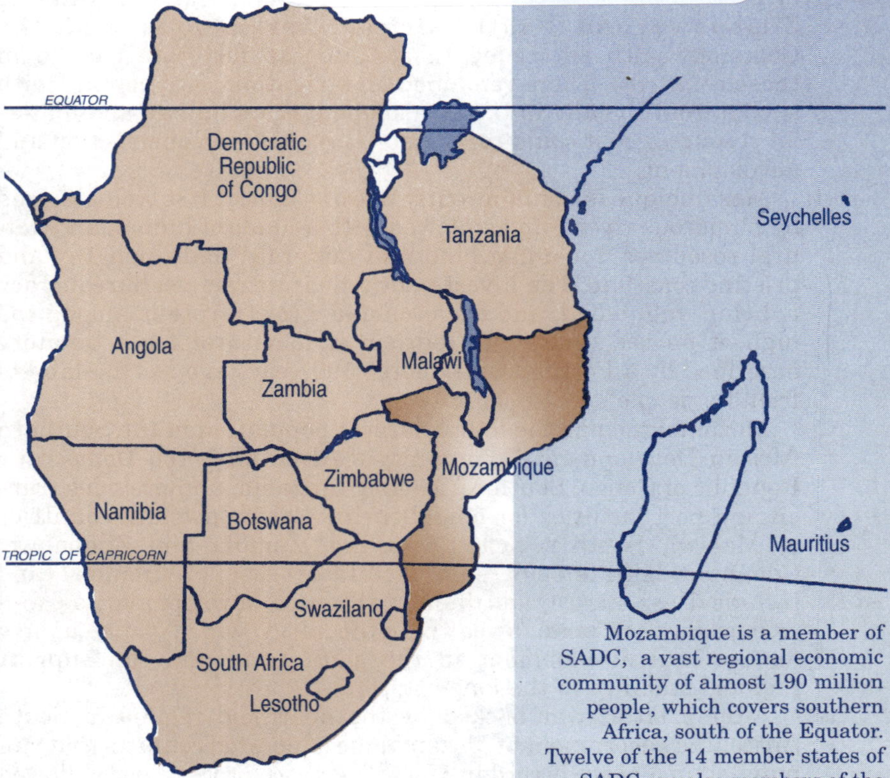

Mozambique is a member of SADC, a vast regional economic community of almost 190 million people, which covers southern Africa, south of the Equator. Twelve of the 14 member states of SADC are also members of the Commonwealth.

Mozambique takes its place as a Commonwealth member at the 1997 Commonwealth Heads of State and Government Meeting (CHOGM) in Edinburgh, Scotland, moving into full membership from its long-time status as a Commonwealth "cousin".

Mozambique's commitment and contribution to Commonwealth ideals and goals was formally recognized a decade ago at the Vancouver CHOGM in 1987, with the establishment of the Special Commonwealth Fund for Mozambique (SCFM), to support its frontline struggle against apartheid in neighbouring South Africa. The SCFM was noteworthy as a Commonwealth programme which attracted financial commitments from developing as well as developed countries.

The strong "exceptional" case for admitting Mozambique to the Commonwealth was defined from the fact that Mozambique's suffering had occurred largely as a result of its support for democracy and human dignity in neighbouring Commonwealth states, ie Zimbabwe and South Africa. Mozambique and the Commonwealth succeeded in assisting to facilitate change in those countries. There remained an obligation to co-operate with such a frontline ally in the development of its human and material resources so it could contribute to regional reconstruction and development.

Mozambique is not inherently a poor country. It is well-watered by numerous rivers, and endowed with abundant human and natural resources, including land and minerals, and a lengthy and pristine coastline. The investment code is attractive, bureaucracy is being unbundled, and the economic growth rate is among the highest on the continent. Tourism is a natural for a territory described by a Portuguese explorer 500 years ago as "the land of friendly people".

Mozambique has the fourth largest population in the Southern African Development Community (SADC) after the Democratic Republic of Congo, South Africa and Tanzania, and provides transit and port facilities for neighbouring Commonwealth countries of Malawi, South Africa, Swaziland, Zambia and Zimbabwe. Commonwealth membership facilitates ease of financial and technical assistance, and human resource development, as well as exposure to Commonwealth methodology, which can be a force for regional development in the short term and can support regional stability in the longer term.

After a bitter war backed by the apartheid regime in South Africa, the government of Mozambique supported contacts that culminated in a peace accord in 1992. The peace process was followed by multi-party elections in 1994 during which two main political parties and a coalition of smaller parties won seats in the National

Assembly. A majority of seats were won by the Frelimo party, and Mozambique ranked eighth in the world (second in the Commonwealth after New Zealand) in its 25.2% representation of women (now 28%).

The winner of the presidential contest among 12 candidates was the Frelimo incumbent who initiated and nurtured the peace process, President Joaquim A. Chissano. He is fluent in English, Tsonga, Portuguese, French, Swahili, and speaks a number of other languages. He was later chosen Deputy Chairman by the 14-member SADC, a community of 190 million people, chaired by President Nelson Mandela.

MOZAMBIQUE

in the Commonwealth

The end of the war, and the forward-looking economic policies implemented by government, have ensured that Mozambique is an attractive investment destination and is no longer labelled by international financial institutions as "the poorest country in the world". This was a definition that excluded the dynamic and creative "informal" sector that operates outside the official economy and statistical base, and is currently being attracted into the mainstream.

Mozambicans share a common dedication to the Commonwealth ideals of equality and dignity, born out of deep human suffering in pursuit of these beliefs. Mozambique is completely surrounded by Commonwealth countries who strongly supported their neighbour's application for membership, which they believe will enhance and advance regional development.

For the southern African region, Mozambique's accession to Commonwealth membership has essential benefits in building its post-apartheid future of regional economic cooperation and integration — through strengthening and expanding the common legacy that exists, facilitating communication and movement of peoples, and encouraging the development of business, trade and investment links.

The government of Mozambique wants to strengthen democracy, develop human resources and infrastructure, and become a contributing partner in regional development, rather than a poor cousin who is a burden on the extended family. In the medium and long term, there is no doubt that Mozambique can make its own contribution to Commonwealth and regional socio-economic and political development.

"The land of friendly people"

MOZAMBIQUE Brief

Head of State	HE Joaquim A. Chissano, also Deputy Chairman of SADC
Prime Minister	Rt. Hon. Dr. Pascoal Mocumbi
Foreign Minister	Hon. Dr. Leonardo Simão
Independence	25 June 1975
Capital City	Maputo
Location	South-east coast of Africa, Indian Ocean coastline
Area	799,390 sq km
Population	Estimate 16.6million (1994), 18million (1997). Projected 19.6million by the year 2000. Approx. 40% of the population lives in two provinces, Nampula and Zambezia. Approx. 33% lives in urban areas.
Census	August 1997, information still being compiled.
Languages	There are 13 national languages and numerous dialects spoken by 11 ethnic groups, and most are shared across boundaries with neighbouring countries. The official language is Portuguese, spoken by about 25% of the population, mainly in cities. English is taught in secondary schools, and is spoken by many young professionals as well as senior government officials and political leaders. Contacts with neighbouring countries at a political and technical level are handled primarily in English.
Religions	African traditional; Christian, both Roman Catholic and Protestant; Muslim; Hindu.
Governance	Executive president, unitary republic, unicameral legislature.
Administrative	Ten provinces plus Maputo city, 128 districts, 23 cities, 387 administrative posts, 68 towns (BIP, 1995).
National Assembly	250 seats, including 70 women (28%)
Last Elections	27-29 October 1994
Memberships	SADC, Organization of African Unity, UN, Commonwealth, Non-Aligned Movement, Organization of the Islamic Conference, Community of Portuguese-Language Countries, Indian Ocean Rim, African-Caribbean-Pacific (ACP) group of signatories to the Lomé Convention with the EU. Mozambique withdrew from the regional trade grouping, Comesa, in early 1997.
Commonwealth	**Mozambique was admitted as a member on 12 November 1995.**

MOZAMBIQUE
The Land

Mozambique mirrors a continent, stretching from the tropical heat of the north and the coast to the subtropical south and the interior, from the flat-topped acacias of the savannah grassland which offer shade to wild animals, to the coastal palms and the mangroves which shelter shellfish. It is a vast and varied land covering most of the south-east coast of Africa, from the Ruvuma river in the north to beyond the Maputo river in the south.

From its northern border with Tanzania to its southern boundary with South Africa, Mozambique is a bridge between east and southern Africa. Three major seaports including the deepest natural harbour on the east African coast, offer a gateway to southern Africa.

Mozambique occupies the southern fringe of the great east African escarpment, and shares one of the Rift-valley lakes, Lake Niassa (Malawi), the world's third deepest lake, containing the highest number of lake-fish species.

Bordering as it does on major bodies of fresh and salt water, the country is generally well-watered, although parts of the south are prone to cyclical droughts. Its territory is crossed by over a dozen main rivers, flowing east to the Indian Ocean. The largest is the Zambezi, the mighty African river which spans the continent from its origins in northwestern Zambia and Angola, filling the giant Cahora Bassa dam in Mozambique's Tete province, before crossing the centre of the country to spill into the ocean.

The mountains of the interior fall to a broad plateau, which covers almost half of the land area, before descending to coastal plains. There are patches of thick forests in the western and northern highlands. The coastal beaches are fringed by lagoons, coral reefs and strings of islands.

The hot, wet season is October to March, when coastal areas are vulnerable to storms and cyclones sweeping in off the sea. From April to September, the coast has warm, mainly dry weather, while the interior highlands shiver in the subtropical cold season.

The land is rich in soils, minerals, vegetation, animals and birdlife. There are four national parks, and many forest and game reserves harbouring zebra, elephants, buffalo, giraffe and a range of tropical water birds, including flamingos and pelicans.

The people of Mozambique are as diverse as their land, from the freshwater fishers of Lake Malawi to the harvesters of the sea, from the rice-growers of the northern coast to the maize-growing inhabitants of the interior, and from the cattle-keepers of the south to the plantation workers of the river valleys, the locomotive engineers, the bank managers, and the urban technocrats.

Languages of Mozambique

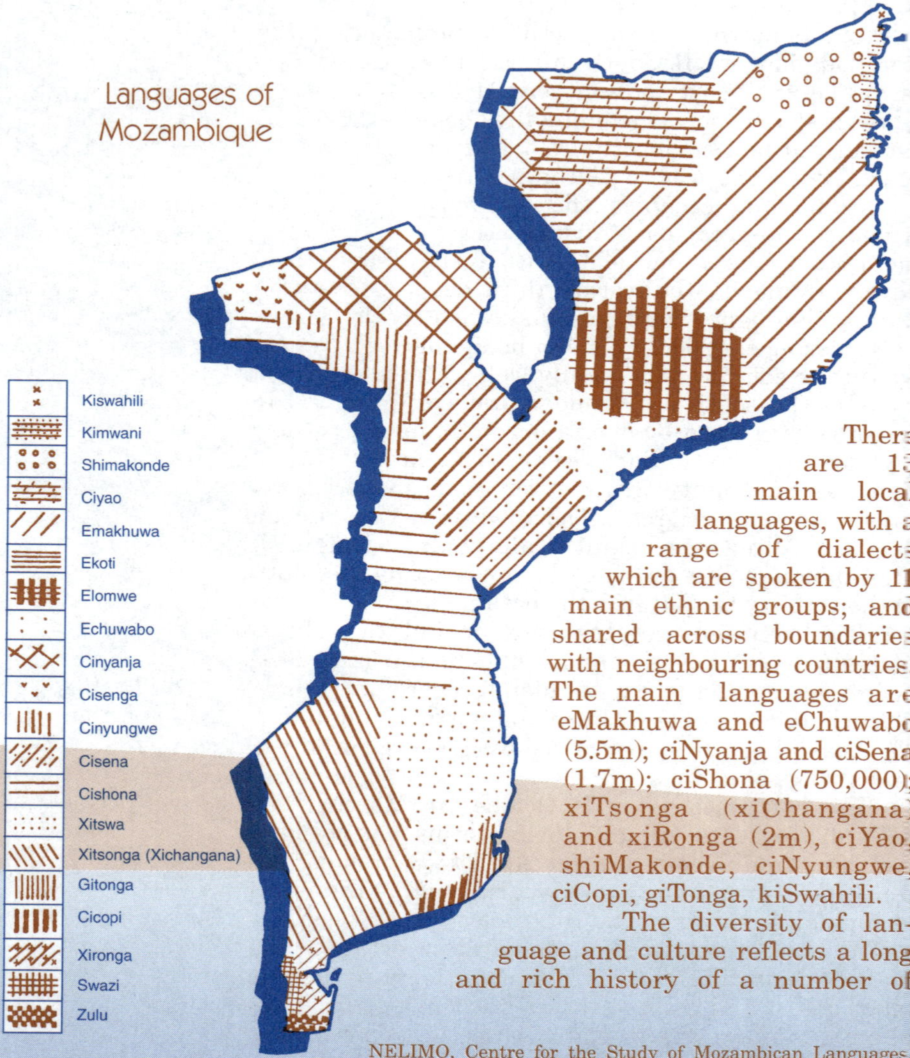

NELIMO, Centre for the Study of Mozambican Languages, Eduardo Mondlane University, 1989

There are 13 main local languages, with a range of dialects which are spoken by 11 main ethnic groups; and shared across boundaries with neighbouring countries. The main languages are eMakhuwa and eChuwabo (5.5m); ciNyanja and ciSena (1.7m); ciShona (750,000); xiTsonga (xiChangana) and xiRonga (2m), ciYao, shiMakonde, ciNyungwe, ciCopi, giTonga, kiSwahili.

The diversity of language and culture reflects a long and rich history of a number of

African civilizations which rose and fell in the centuries before the seaports were plied by Arab traders, before the penetration of the river valleys by Portuguese priests and entrepreneurs. When the Portuguese explorer, Vasco da Gama, arrived on the coast of Inhambane at the end of the 15th century, he found a dynamic society with trading links to the African hinterland and to the Middle East and China. Coastal Mozambique was proclaimed a Portuguese colony in the mid-18th century, with its capital in the north, at Ilha de Moçambique. With the partition of Africa by the European powers at the end of the 19th century, Portugal's army finally consolidated Lisbon's control over a larger area that is now Mozambique, but the last pockets of African military resistance were subdued only in the first quarter of the 20th century.

Resistance resumed midway through the 20th century, and the various nationalist and anti-colonialist groups were united in 1962 as the Mozambique Liberation Front (Frelimo), under the leadership of Dr Eduardo Mondlane. When attempts to negotiate independence failed, Frelimo launched an armed liberation struggle in 1964, which ended in a transition to independence a decade later.

Dr Mondlane was assassinated in 1969, with a book bomb sent by the Portuguese secret police. Samora Machel was elected the second President of Frelimo, and became the first President of independent Mozambique. His Prime Minister during the transition to independence in 1974 was Joaquim Chissano, later elected the third president of Frelimo after President Machel and some of his key advisors were killed in a still unexplained plane crash in South African territory in 1986. Mozambique has never closed its inquiry into the cause of that plane crash, widely believed to have been caused by a false beacon which lured the plane off course into the hills at Mbuzini, South Africa.

Mozambique gained its political independence from Portugal on 25 June 1975, after a nine-month transitional period, following an agreement signed in Zambia. Under the Salazar dictatorship in Portugal, Mozambique had been considered a "province", and independence was not granted easily. A nationalist independence movement grew out of the students' movement and among political prisoners, before three parties united to form Frelimo, which took up arms in 1964. The transition to independence was negotiated a decade later, after the liberation wars in Africa had precipitated a coup d'etat in Portugal in April 1974.

Mozambique closed its border with Southern Rhodesia in 1976, in compliance with international sanctions, and at great cost to its economy which was reliant on transit revenues for use of ports and railways. The initial cost estimate was US$510 million up to 1980, but the economic and political impact was far greater. Southern Rhodesia retaliated with direct military force, and through establishing and training a clandestine military intelligence group, the Mozambique National Resistance, which moved to South Africa when Zimbabwe became independent in 1980, and later established itself as a political-military party, now Renamo, with support in the centre and north of the country.

Using direct sabotage of road and rail links, in addition to Renamo activities, South Africa managed to control access to Commonwealth countries of the interior by destroying transport links through Mozambique. At least four Commonwealth countries gave military assistance to Mozambique, with troops, equipment, logistics or training. After South Africa bombed three Commonwealth capitals (Gaborone, Harare, Lusaka) in 1986, signalling the end of the Commonwealth Mission to South Africa, the war in Mozambique escalated.

After informal contacts initiated by the churches, and following two years of protracted negotiations in Rome, a peace accord was signed in October 1992, marking the start of a UN-monitored peace process, which lasted another two years. By the time Mozambique held national elections in October 1994, its old adversary of apartheid had been defeated, and South Africa had held its own democratic elections.

In the elections in Mozambique, the Frelimo presidential candidate, Joaquim Chissano, was elected with a majority in the first round, and Frelimo won a clear majority of seats in the National Assembly (Parliament). The results were close, and three parties gained seats on a proportional representation system based on provincial lists: Frelimo 44.33% (129 seats), Renamo 33.78% (112 seats), and the Democratic Union 5.15% (9 seats).

Frelimo's decision that one-third of its candidates would be women, ensured a representation of women in the National Assembly of 25.2% (now 28%). Mozambique and other SADC leaders have since signed a regional Gender Declaration (1997) that commits them to a 30 percent target of women in political and decision-making structures by the year 2005.

Mozambique is a unitary republic with ten provinces plus Maputo city, 128 districts, 23 cities, 387 administrative posts and 68 towns (BIP, 1995). Under a decentralized programme of state administration, local elections will be phased in, with elections planned in 33 municipal districts before mid-1998. However, more difficult than organizing the elections, is the implementation of the systems that follow, the division of power and the collection and management of resources at municipal level.

MOZAMBIQUE

Political System and Governance

The 1990 constitution provides for Mozambicans to exercise their political rights through "electing their representatives by universal, direct, secret and periodic suffrage, through referenda on major national issues and through permanent democratic participation by citizens in the affairs of the nation". The constitution provides for a multi-party political system, a market-based economy, and the separation of executive, legislative and judicial powers. The official organs of sovereign authority are the President of the Republic, the Assembly of the Republic (Parliament), the Council of Ministers, the Courts and the Constitutional Council.

The 1990 constitution abolished the death penalty, and affirmed the right to strike. Freedom of movement is protected, and conservation and preservation of the environment is provided for.

The fundamental constitutional aims include the consolidation of national unity, social justice, material and spiritual wellbeing of citizens, human rights and the equality of citizens before the law, strengthening of democracy, economic and scientific progress, traditional social and cultural values, and developing friendly relations with other people and states.

The government defines its current goals as the consolidation of peace, stability and unity; reducing the level of absolute poverty and wiping it out over the medium term; improving living conditions, education, health, rural development and employment.

GOVERNANCE
unitary republic
executive president
council of ministers
unicameral multi-party legislature
judiciary, courts
constitutional council

NATIONAL ASSEMBLY
250 seats,
70 women (28%)

LAST ELECTIONS
October 1994

NEXT ELECTIONS
local, 1997/98
national, 1999

MOZAMBIQUE Economic indicators

GNP per capita (excluding informal sector)	US$120
Total GDP (excluding informal sector)	US$1.5billion
agriculture, forestry, fisheries % of GDP	33%
industry % of GDP	12%
services % of GDP	55%
Consumption % of GDP	
private	75%
government	20%
Real GDP growth estimate (1996)	6%
Inflation (1996)	18%
Total external debt (1995)	US$5.781billion

Employment

Percent of labour force in	
agriculture	83%
industry	8%
services	9%
Women in labour force	48%

Trade

Export earnings (1995)	US$170 million
Imports (1995)	US$784 million
Exports as % of imports	22%
Main exports	Prawns, US$70 million/year (almost half export revenue); cotton, cashew nuts and copra
Main imports	Machinery, raw materials, consumer goods, food
Main trading partners	
exports	Spain, South Africa, India, Japan, Portugal
imports	South Africa, Zimbabwe, Saudi Arabia, Portugal

Currency	The metical is now freely floated
Exchange	US$=11,428 meticais, Aug 1997

MOZAMBIQUE

Macro-Economic and Finance

Mozambique is defined by international financial institutions as a "low income country", which is currently dependent on aid, due to the aftermath of war, drought and chronic underdevelopment dating from colonial times. The vulnerable economy inherited at independence rested on income from ports and railways, and from migrant labourers working in South Africa with partial remittance for their labour paid to the State in gold. The post-independence period saw a marked improvement in the country's socio-economic outlook, and considerable progress was made in the first six years, with all indicators on the rise. Agricultural and mineral exports increased; school enrolment tripled, and health care was hailed as a model. Then came the apartheid-backed war which disrupted or destroyed infrastructure including roads and railways, farms and agro-industrial complexes, aid projects, schools, health clinics and rural shops; and cost the country well over US$20 billion, including GDP loss.

There is an extensive programme of reconstruction underway, and in 1996, the Paris Club agreed under the Naples Agreement to write off two-thirds of the foreign debt incurred from 1975-1984, with the remainder to be paid over 20 years. New proposals have been made recently concerning 80 percent.

The international donor community provided more than US$8 billion from 1987-1995, in grants, credits and debt relief. Main bilateral donors are Germany, Italy, Sweden, US and Norway. The World Bank and IMF have shown confidence in the economic future of the country, and further aid from Canada, Sweden and the European Union was agreed in early 1997.

An economic rehabilitation programme (PRE) was launched in 1987, aimed at undercutting the unofficial economy, giving real value to the currency, and removing administrative hindrances to productive enterprises.

Privatisation is a foundation of the economic recovery programme, and government has already sold its interest in almost 700 companies, although the pace of the exercise and the dearth of available local capital has caused some concerns over possible foreign control of the economy. There are two privatisation agencies. UTRE handles large industries; small and medium-sized industries and tourism go through GREI.

Technical Unit for Enterprise Restructuring (UTRE),
CP 4350, Maputo

Office for Restructuring of Industrial, Commercial and Tourism Enterprises (GREI)
Av 25 Setembro 1167, Maputo
Tel (258-1) 42 38 34
Fax (258-1) 42 85 80

Fisheries

Prawns and shrimps are the major export at 14,000t/year, with sustainable annual catch estimated at 500,000t of fish (300,000t anchovies, the rest mainly mackerel). Japan, Spain, Portugal and South Africa participate in the fishing industry, through joint ventures or direct licensing.

Agriculture

Once the world's largest producer of cashew nuts, production has fallen in recent years (to 29,400t in 1994), now increasing. Sugar cane (234,000t) and raw cotton (49,000t) were produced for export in 1994; also copra, sisal and tea. Maize is an important domestic market crop (146,000t in 1994). Horticulture is significant; rice and beans, as well as tobacco, coconuts and citrus.

Forestry

There are about 19 million hectares of productive woodland, from eucalyptus and pine to rare hardwoods. Timber production declined during the war, and export earnings fell in this sector. The country's largest timber project at Ifloma, in Manica province, is producing below capacity.

Mining

Minerals accounted for just three percent of total exports in 1993. This sector's potential has been hampered by insecurity, obsolete equipment and transport difficulties, which can now be resolved. Known main reserves: nepheline syenite (for aluminium), iron ore, apatite, magnetite, graphite and marble. Others include tantalite and other pegmatites, copper, garnet, kaolin, asbestos, bentonite, limestone, gold, titanium, bauxite and tin.

Manufacturing

The industrial base is small but growing. Output of textiles and clothing, pharmaceuticals and electrical equipment declined, due to shortage of raw materials and inability to compete with imported products, but has been boosted by peace, economic liberalization and provision of incentives.

Light industries: food-processing, textiles, brewing, cement, soap.

Energy

Potential energy exporter, especially electricity; large gas reserves, and coal potential. Some river basins are of interest to oil prospectors, especially Rovuma, Zambezi and Limpopo. A domestic energy programme aims to reduce timber consumption and promote gas, paraffin and coal. Known reserves: coal (10,000 million t); Pande natural gasfield (40,000million cu m); may be significant petroleum. Cahora Bassa is Africa's second largest hydroelectric plant, now exporting to South Africa and Zimbabwe.

Tourism

This is a potential growth area for a country which has everything: 2,500 km of Indian Ocean beaches, coral reefs, diving, deep-sea fishing, wildlife and game parks, highlands and plains. Infrastructure is being redefined, planning and reconstruction are underway.

Transport

The transport sector is a key element in Mozambique's economy. The ports of Beira, Maputo and Nacala are the closest outlets to the sea for neighbouring countries, and these transport corridors have potential in a broader development context.

TRADE, INVESTMENT AND DEVELOPMENT

The Road to Commonwealth Prosperity

Foreign investment has been directed mainly towards mining and energy, privatisation of the transport infrastructure and farming activities. A number of guarantees and incentives, including tax holidays, are offered to foreign investors, and joint ventures between local business and foreign investors are encouraged. The government is attempting to reduce the complexity of its investment laws, and industrial tax-free zones are being developed.

Foreign investment is regulated by the 1993 Investment Law, which provides that all investment projects should be proposed to and approved by the Investment Promotion Centre. The investment law defines government objectives as:

to stimulate regional development, expand capacity and satisfy local demand; increase the tax base, create jobs and raise skill levels; promote management skills; develop the national infrastructure; increase and diversify exports; reduce imports through substitution; and attract foreign currency.

Investors are guaranteed the right to remit profits abroad and repatriate capital. Property rights, ownership and entrepreneurial freedom are protected. A flexible tariff code provides for the duty free importation of equipment used in feasibility studies, building materials and equipment. Raw materials, components and packaging to be used in the first production cycle can also be imported with no tariff. Equity capital can be imported freely, while profits of foreign investors, royalties, loan repayments and proceeds through the sale of capital equipment can be exported. Expenditure allowable to be set against tax includes the construction or rehabilitation of public infrastructure and the training of Mozambican workers.

The 1993 law enables the establishment of Industrial Free Zones (IFZs), to be developed by the private sector, with at least 85 percent of output to be for export. Zone developers should invest US$5 million and will be exempted from paying taxes and customs duties, although a royalty fee of one percent of turnover will be payable from the sixth year of operation. Firms operating from an IFZ should invest over

$50,000 and will be exempt from taxes and customs duties. A one percent royalty is payable from the second year of operation.

The Investment Law does not favour any particular economic sector, but contains geographic incentives. Investment in a new or rehabilitated institution within a provincial capital, for example, attracts a reduction of 50 percent in industrial contribution tax and supplementary tax for up to 10 years; investment outside provincial capitals attracts a 65 percent reduction; investment in the northern provinces of Niassa, Cabo Delgado and Tete will attract 80 percent reduction.

There is considerable potential for investment in infrastructure, as well as the largely unexploited natural resources, such as forests, minerals and fossil fuels.

The main areas of economic growth all require the completion of significant construction projects, so construction is one of the leading magnets for investment.

In the tourism sector, the infrastructure, training, accommodation, and the construction of tourist attractions all require investment.

The most significant investors are Portugal, South Africa, Britain and Hong Kong.

Min. Industry, Commerce and Tourism,
Praça 25 de Junho,
CP 1831, Maputo
Tel (258-1) 42 60 91
42 72 04
Fax (258-1) 42 13 51

National Directorate of Tourism,
Av 25 Setembro 1203,
Maputo
Tel (258-1) 42 17 94
Fax (258-1) 42 17 95

Investment Promotion Centre,
Av 25 Setembro 2049,
1st floor, CP 4635,
Maputo
Tel (258-1) 42 24 56/7
Fax (258-1) 42 24 59

Chamber of Commerce,
rua Mateus Sensão Mutemba 452,
CP 1836, Maputo
Tel (258-1) 49 19 70

Laws governing investment

Investment Law 1993	provides that all investment projects should be proposed to and approved by the Investment Promotion Centre.
Mining Law 1985	covers investment in prospecting for mineral resources.
Petroleum Law 1981	covers investment in prospecting for oil, gas.
Tourism Four-Year Plan	outlines 19 areas, or Tourism Partial Protection Zones, where tourism development has priority; and provides that this must be co-ordinated with other government programmes and take into account environmental factors.

MOZAMBIQUE

SADC Region

Regional development is not new to the people of this land, who have been involved for centuries in long-distance trade and development of the interior.

For the past century — since the British entrepreneur Cecil Rhodes, South African Boer trekkers and Portuguese settlers argued over access to Delagoa Bay (now Maputo) — Mozambique has provided transport infrastructure, as a transit economy based on earnings from services provided to its landlocked neighbours.

Mozambicans have also assisted in development of neighbouring countries for the past 100 years through their labour, as migrants to the mines and plantations in South Africa, Zimbabwe, Malawi, Tanzania.

Government and private sector together are promoting the country as a gateway to the southern African market through the Maputo and Beira "development corridors", respectively, to South Africa and Zimbabwe. These corridors are more than transport routes, although they follow the lines of road and rail, connecting the port cities to the hinterland. They are planned as "development corridors" to attract investment for commercial, manufacturing and service industries, including tourism.

Rehabilitation of ports and railways has been underway for some years, especially for Beira where traffic has been increasing since 1990, and for Nacala, reopened in 1993. Rehabilitation of main roads is underway, and the proposed Maputo development corridor is expected to facilitate rapid rehabilitation of the southern route.

Three major seaports, including the deepest natural harbour on the east African coast at Nacala, offer a gateway to southern Africa, for Australia, for India, Malaysia, Sri Lanka, and other Asian countries to the east, and for the Middle East and Europe to the north.

The Cahora Bassa dam is another example of regional development potential. Originally designed to supply electricity to South Africa, it is now supplying Zimbabwe, whose grid is connected to the Democratic Republic of Congo, South Africa and Zambia.

Mozambique plays an active role in the SADC, hosting the transport and communications commission (SATCC) and the sector for culture and information. President Chissano is Deputy Chairman of SADC.

MOZAMBIQUE
Selected Human Development Indicators*

Education	
Literacy	40%
Enrolment (combined first and second level gross enrolment ratio)	35%
Compulsory education	7 years
Higher education as % of all levels	10%
Population under 15 years of age	46%
under 30 years of age	+70%
Health	
Population growth rate	2.7%
Life expectancy at birth	46 years
Access to health services	39%
safe water	63%
sanitation	54%
Infant mortality rate 116/1,000 live births	
Gender	
Women in Parliament	25.2%
Women in Government	13%
Administrators/Managers	11.3%
Literacy	22.1%

While the Human Development Indicators for Mozambique remain low, it is no longer the "poorest" country in the world, and the indicators continue to rise. In the gender indicators developed by the UNDP, Mozambique gets a much higher rating in both gender-related development and gender empowerment. However, the literacy rate remains much lower for women than men, at 22 percent.

The 1990 constitution states that, "All citizens are equal before the law. They shall enjoy the same rights, and shall be subject to the same duties regardless of colour, race, sex, ethnic origin, place of birth, religion, educational level, social position, the legal status of their parents, or their profession.

"Men and women shall be equal before the law in all spheres of political, economic, social and cultural affairs."

* HDI figures are for 1994, from UNDP's *Human Development Report 1997*

Education is a priority area for government, followed by health care and other services such as water and housing. Adult literacy is about 40 percent, due to extensive educational and literacy campaigns over the past 20 years which raised the figure from seven percent at independence. Literacy levels could have risen higher but for the war which targeted the destruction of schools and health clinics. Mozambique had well over 5,000 primary schools in the early 1980s, of which 70 percent were destroyed or disrupted. However, since 1994, an active reconstruction programme has rebuilt them.

There are 5,600 primary schools, and enrolment now stands at 1.75 million, with a target of 6,000 schools and 1.9 million primary students by 1998.

Portuguese is the official language of instruction, but local languages are increasingly being used at primary level. English has been taught at secondary schools dating back to colonial times and as a policy since independence.

Enrolment at tertiary level still numbers only a few thousand, with about one quarter women. As well as the Eduardo Mondlane University in Maputo, there are two other state-supported institutions, and four private universities, including a Roman Catholic university with campuses in Beira and Nampula.

As with the education sector, the broad-based primary health-care system and its rural health facilities, which covered at least 81 percent of rural children, were targeted during the war. Additional deaths caused by disruption of the health facilities were estimated at over one million, through increased infant and child mortality, diarrhoea and curable diseases.

By 1990, about half of the basic health posts had been destroyed or closed, and 996 remained operational, with 226 health centres, 26 rural hospitals, seven provincial hospitals, three central hospitals and two psychiatric hospitals.

About 17 percent of the national budget is devoted to education, and eight percent to health. By the time the peace accord was signed in late 1992, there were well over 1.5 million refugees in neigbouring countries and at least 4.5 million people displaced within the country. Five years later, most have returned home and are being resettled.

The task of reconstruction has begun, but it is a massive task that involves not only the distribution of seeds, hoes and building materials but also landmine clearance in a countryside that may have as many as two million landmines in its soil.

The majority of the labour force are engaged in agriculture, mostly subsistence or informal. Of the recorded waged labour force, almost half were employed in industry and 20 percent in transport. There is a minimum wage in both urban and rural areas; and the right to strike is legalized under the 1990 constitution. Public sector wages take up over 50 percent of government expenditure, but wages have declined substantially in real terms since 1991.

Large numbers of Mozambicans continue to work outside the country, mostly men who are employed as migrant workers in South Africa's mines, industries and farms. In 1996, 57,000 Mozambicans were officially employed in the South African mines, although the number working illegally is thought to be several times higher.

There is a lively non-governmental sector in Mozambique, and civil society organs are becoming increasingly visible, especially the umbrella organisations such as the Christian Council of Mozambique, and Forum Mulher (The Forum of Women). Many rural non-governmental organisations (NGOs) and community-based organisations (CBOs) work in agriculture, health, and provision of assistance and facilities for the streets kids who are numerous on city streets, especially in Maputo. There is an independent liaison office for both local and foreign NGOs in Maputo, called LINK.

Eduardo Mondlane University,
Office of the Rector
Praça 25 de Junho,
37 — 4th floor,
PO Box 257, Maputo
Tel (258-1) 42 86 82
43 02 39
42 59 76
Fax (258-1) 42 64 26

Ordem dos Advogados
(Law Society)
Av V Lenin, 691
1st floor, Maputo
Tel (258-1) 43 16 34
43 16 36

Forum Mulher
(Forum of Women)
Rua Pereira do Lago,
147, 6th floor,
PO Box 3632, Maputo
Tel (258-1) 49 27 45
Fax (258-1) 49 34 37

LINK NGO Forum
Rua Mariano
Machado, 56,
Bairro Central,
PO Box 2187, Maputo
Tel (258-1) 30 17 81,
30 20 34,
Fax (258-1) 30 19 18/9
Email
forum@link.uem.mz

MOZAMBIQUE

Culture Sport

One of the fundamental aims of the Republic of Mozambique, as set out in the 1990 constitution, is the affirmation of the Mozambican character, its traditions and other social and cultural values; and the government has established culture centres in every province.

The constitution recognizes the value of national languages and assures the promotion of "their development and increased role as languages which are used in the daily life and education of its citizens".

The arts — including music and dance, theatre, painting and sculpture, and crafts — are lively, innovative and dynamic. Mozambique has produced some of the continent's finest artists, the best known being the sculptors Chissano, Zaqueu and Ndlozy, the painter Malangatana, and others such as Naguib, Ubisse, Samate, Shikani, Cossa and Chichorro.

Film-making has been innovative, with many joint productions, and there is a professional Photographic Training Centre run by one of the country's leading photographers, Ricardo Rangel. The Centre also maintains a commercial photographic archive containing the works of many local photographers and covering all sectors.

Mozambique has responsibility for coordinating the SADC sector for culture and information which is establishing a regional data base on culture, and drafting a regional information policy. In June 1997, Mozambique hosted the first SADC Theatre Festival.

Sport is as varied as culture in Mozambique, including soccer, athletics, deep-sea fishing, swimming and diving, and golf, among others. The country has qualified for the third time to the Africa Cup of Nations; and the country's first Olympic medal was won by the "Maputo Express" Maria de Lurdes Mutola at the 1996 Olympic Games in Atlanta, when she won a bronze in the 800-metres. She won another bronze in Athens, in the same event at the World Athletics Championships.

The constitution guarantees that, "citizens shall have the right to physical education and sport. The State shall promote, through sporting and educational institutions, the practise and dissemination of physical education and sport."

Malangatana

Ministry of Culture,
Youth and Sports,
Av Patrice Lumumba,
1217, CP 1742,
Maputo
Tel (258-1) 42 00 68/72
Fax (258-1) 42 00 97
Telex 6621 CULT

MOZAMBIQUE

Media

Radio Moçambique (RM) is the national radio, broadcasting in 10 local languages as well as Portuguese, with an external service in English. As well as the national service, RM operates a Maputo city radio station. Three private radio stations operate on FM in Maputo, with a fourth one in the planning stages by a journalists' cooperative, and one in the northern city of Nampula.

There are two television stations in Maputo, TVM and RTK. TVM is the national television, which also broadcasts in Beira and Nampula, with plans to extend to other northern capitals.

There are two daily newspapers: *Noticias* in Maputo, with a circulation of about 30,000; and *Diario de Moçambique* in Beira, circ. 16,000. Weekly newspapers — *Savana, Domingo, Demos* and *Fin de Semana* — publish on Friday, Sunday, Wednesday, Thursday, respectively. *Savana* is owned by a cooperative of 13 journalists established in 1992, called Mediacoop. Its first publication was a three-page *Mediafax* newsletter, distributed by fax. This innovation has caught on in Maputo, and there are now five newsletters distributed by fax. There are two weekly newspapers devoted to sports.

The national news agency, AIM, provides a news service domestically and outside the country in both Portuguese and English. Its publication *Telinforma* is circulated electronically in English.

Freedom of the press is guaranteed under the constitution, including "in particular the freedom of journalistic expression and creativity, access to sources of information, protection of professional independence and confidentiality, and the right to publish newspapers and other publications."

Presentation of Mozambique in the foreign media has been generally negative, often portrayed by relief agencies for fund-raising purposes. Since the end of the war in 1992, most foreign news agencies do not send correspondents to Mozambique, and very little reporting is being done on development issues, including the economic upturn in the years since the peace accord. Travel writers visit Mozambique occasionally, and focus on the attractions and potential for tourism.

Sousa

National Union
of Journalists,
Av 24 de Julho, 231,
Maputo
Tel (258-1) 49 25 00
Fax (258-1) 42 20 31

MOZAMBIQUE

A Shared Historical Experience

Completely surrounded by Commonwealth members, and used in colonial times as a transit route for these countries (then colonies), it was out of a deep moral obligation as well as geopolitical considerations, that post-independence Mozambique assumed a vocal and active leadership role in the region against the rebel regime in Southern Rhodesia and apartheid in South Africa. Later, a number of Commonwealth countries provided military or peacekeeping assistance to Mozambique, as well as training and materials.

Mozambique, therefore, shares a common historical experience with neighbouring countries and other Commonwealth members, most recently:

- in actively opposing the illegal declaration of independence in Southern Rhodesia, with resultant defence costs, loss of life and infrastructure due to Rhodesian military attacks, culminating in the indepedence of Zimbabwe, a goal the Commonwealth was also pursuing; and
- in actively opposing apartheid, on both diplomatic and military fronts, in a manner that hastened the change in South Africa and which the new South African government has publicly acknowledged. President Mandela's first external visit was to Mozambique, and the first leader from the region to pay a state visit to South Africa was President Chissano in early 1995.

Mozambique's role was acknowledged in the South African Parliament in Cape Town when the people of South Africa apologized formally to the people of Mozambique for the suffering and destruction caused during the fight against apartheid.

President Chissano responded, with typical Mozambican understatement, that they were only doing what had to be done, that they had suffered together, and that there was no need to apologize.

"Mozambique has stood at the forefront in the struggle for democracy and human rights here in southern Africa, steadfastly opposing racist minority government in what was once called Rhodesia and against apartheid in South Africa. For its principled commitment to these values, Mozambique has paid a tremendous cost in human and material terms."

Commonwealth Secretary-General, Chief Emeka Anyaoku, Maputo, February 1991

MOZAMBIQUE

A Special Political Relationship

Mozambique has had a special relationship with the Commonwealth for over 30 years, since Tanzania provided the rear base for its liberation struggle and subsequently, together with Zambia, hosted negotiations for the 1974 transition to independence. In 1976, the year after independence, Mozambique closed its lengthy and lucrative border with Southern Rhodesia in compliance with international sanctions initiated by the Commonwealth. In 1979, the then President Samora Machel gave assistance which the British Prime Minister, Margaret Thatcher, considered critical and courageous, in helping her to resolve the "Rhodesia problem", handing her a very early foreign policy victory and broadening her perpsective on possible solutions.

Mozambique sent a ministerial delegation to Lusaka for the Commonwealth summit in 1979 and, later that year, towards the end of the Lancaster House talks, when agreement had been reached on the holding of general elections with full adult suffrage, President Machel sent a personal message encouraging the nationalist delegations to settle an outstanding issue. The British government's view of Machel as a courageous leader was reinforced in 1984 when he signed the Nkomati Accord with South Africa (which the latter soon abrogated).

Canada, Australia and New Zealand developed special bilateral relationships with Mozambique during the apartheid era, as did several Commonwealth developing and newly industrialised countries who contributed through the Special Commonwealth Fund for Mozambique (SCFM), or bilaterally. SCFM provided technical assistance to Mozambique from 1988-94, with scholarships, institutional and human resource development particularly to Eduardo Mondlane University, English language training, telecommunications, agricultural and rural development, marketing and export market development, industrial development for factory managers, and small projects. SCFM was replaced in 1994 by the Commonwealth Capacity-Building Facility for Mozambique, a programme of technical cooperation with AusAID, Australia.

The above represents the common purpose of human dignity and equality, and opposition to racism, values at the heart of the modern Commonwealth.

SCFM and bilateral contributors: Africa Fund Australia, Barbados, Bahamas, Botswana, Britain, Canada, Cyprus, Ghana, Guyana, India, Malaysia, Malta, New Zealand, Nigeria, Pakistan, St. Kitts & Nevis, Samoa, Sierra Leone, Singapore, Swaziland, Tanzania, Trinidad & Tobago, Uganda, Zambia and Zimbabwe.

For the southern African region, Mozambique's accession to Commonwealth membership has essential benefits in building a post-apartheid future of regional economic cooperation and integration – through strengthening and expanding the common legacy that exists, facilitating communication and movement of peoples, and encouraging the development of business, trade and investment links.

Language

Ability to communicate in the English language has been a policy priority for Mozambique for over 20 years, since English was made a compulsory subject in secondary schools soon after Independence in 1975, and most senior government officials and political leaders speak English fluently. Contacts with neighbouring countries at a political and technical level are handled primarily in English.

Education

Mozambicans have benefited from training in various Commonwealth countries, and continue to require assistance with human resource development, which can be facilitated largely through institutions in neighbouring countries. The educational system in Mozambique is currently being revised, and would benefit from multilingual Commonwealth models, particularly in neighbouring countries, such as Zimbabwe, Namibia and South Africa.

Usage of English and the planned introduction of local languages in the early grades also facilitates sharing of human and financial resources and exchange of books with neighbouring countries.

There are seven institutions of higher learning, of which three are state funded and four are private. University level development would benefit from expertise and exchanges with Commonwealth universities, including those which can offer a bilingual model.

Public Administration

This is the area with the least legacy in common with other Commonwealth members, but the greatest need for technical assistance and human resource development and exchange. It is also a key area in which synchronization will greatly benefit regional relations and development. In addition, it is an area in which Mozambique can share its own experiences and expertise with its neighbours, being able to give as well as take advice on this subject, for example, in the area of grassroots decision-making. Other Commonwealth African models can be studied, such as the strong cultural base of local government in Botswana.

State administration, as it heads into local government elections, could benefit from Commonwealth expertise in this regard – just as a very small Commonwealth technical mission established the technical and financial framework for national elections.

Mozambique can also benefit from Commonwealth technical assistance in establishing a Public Service Commission to administer appointments to the public service. Once established, this body can benefit from close consultation with similar Commonwealth institutions, thus facilitating greater contact and exchange between officials.

The establishment of this institution with Commonwealth assistance would facilitate regional cooperation and smoother exchange with officials and professionals at all levels of government in the various neighbouring countries. The British government is facilitating a technical study in this area.

Legal and Parliamentary Affairs

Mozambique is intent on strengthening its parliamentary democracy and the judiciary, and looks forward to further exposure to Commonwealth methodology in this regard. Each member of the Southern African Development Community (SADC), while inheriting some features of a colonial model in common, has developed its own parliamentary system, according to its own situation and requirements. Mozambique will benefit from exchanges with neighbouring countries through the emerging SADC Parliamentary Forum, and from wider bilateral exposure within the Commonwealth.

This is also the case with the strengthening of the judiciary, particularly since each country in the region inherited its own unique system (and in some cases, a separate legal basis such as Roman-Dutch law for Zimbabwe and South Africa).

Visas/Free Movement of People and Goods

This is a priority area for SADC, without which trade and commerce cannot prosper. It is a complex subject when it comes to implementation, but one which the Commonwealth in general has overcome (with some exceptions) in the case of free movement of peoples.

"Among those countries which are members of the Commonwealth, business travel and other non-permanent movement of persons is relatively unproblematic," says one SADC document. "However, movement to and from countries which are not Commonwealth members is often a time-consuming process."

This also impacts on the so-called "brain drain" in the region, whereby expertise could be shared and could move more easily between countries in southern Africa according to their particular development needs, without being seen as "draining" from its country of origin. This may increase short-term pressure on South Africa, which is already facing the problem of migrant labourers and illegal immigrants, although there would have to be other checks and balances to prevent abuse (as there are in Europe).

The main point here is that the sooner the Mozambican economy can be stable and growing, then the more likely Mozambicans will be able to find jobs at home rather than in neighbouring countries. Commonwealth membership can play an important role in this regard, through investment and trade, technical assistance, and development of human and financial resources.

Conflict Resolution

Mozambique has considerable experience in conflict resolution and reconciliation which it can bring to regional and international relations, and can work with its neighbours in ending illegal cross-border activities, smuggling of lethal items including weapons and drugs, and non-lethal items, such as foodstuffs, spare parts, vehicles and electrical equipment.

The contribution to regional stability will become apparent as Mozambique becomes part of a wider network of relations based on common methodology and institutions.

Mozambique is multi-ethnic, as are most other members of the Commonwealth, and can share in this experience of building a modern state and a stable nation, through institutions such as the Commonwealth Parliamentary Association (CPA). For this and a number of other reasons, Mozambique can benefit from, and contribute to, debate on multi-ethnicity through closer relations with Commonwealth countries such as Malaysia, South Africa, India and Canada.

Shared Ideals

Mozambique's adherence to the Commonwealth's non-racial ideals of equality and common humanity is beyond question. Mozambicans have paid for these ideals with their blood, their children and the life of their first president, and they bring with them their own fierce dedication to justice and human equality.

MOZAMBIQUE Other Contacts

Mozambique High Commissions

KENYA	Hughes Building, 4th floor, Kenyatta Ave, P.O.Box 66923, Nairobi Tel (254-2) 221 979 Fax (254-2) 222 446
MALAWI	Commercial Bank Building, Lilongwe Tel (265)784 100, 784 696 Fax (265) 781 342
SOUTH AFRICA	199 Beckett Street, Arcadia 0083, P.O.Box 40750, Pretoria 0002 Tel (27-12) 343-7840 Fax (27-12) 343-6714
SWAZILAND	Highlands View, Princess Drive Road, P.O. Box 1212, Mbabane Tel (268) 43700 Fax 43692
TANZANIA	25-25A Garden Avenue, Box 9370, Dar es Salaam Tel (255-51)33062/5 Fax (255-51) 41136/7
UNITED KINGDOM	21 Fitzroy Square, London W1P 5HJ Tel (44-171) 383-3800 Fax (44-171) 383-3801
ZAMBIA	P.O. Box 34877, Lusaka Tel (260-1) 239 135, 220 333 Fax (260-1) 220 345
ZIMBABWE (and BOTSWANA)	152 Herbert Chitepo Ave, P.O. Box 4608, Harare Tel (263-4) 790 837/9 Fax (263-4) 732 898

Embassies with links to Commonwealth Countries

UNITED NATIONS	70 East 79th Street, New York, NY 10021, USA Tel (1-212) 517-4550/3 Fax (1-212) 734-308
WASHINGTON (and CANADA)	1990 M Street NW, Suite 570, Washington DC 20036, USA Tel (1-202) 239-7146/9 Fax (1-202) 835-0245

Further Reading

Commonwealth Trade and Investment Almanac, 1997
The Commonwealth Yearbook, 1997
Investment Opportunities in Mozambique, 1996
Legislation on Investment in Mozambique, CPI
Strategy for the Development of Tourism in Mozambique
Investment in Mozambique's Tourism Sector, CPI
Investment in Mozambique's Agricultural Sector, CPI
Mineral Resources Development and Investment Opportunities
Mozambique: Land of Peace and Promise, BIP, 1996
Mozambiquefile (monthly) and Telinforma (weekly), AIM
Mozambique Chronology, SARDC, 1990-97
Apartheid Terrorism, Commonwealth Secretariat, 1989

Ministry of Foreign Affairs,
Av Julius Nyerere, 4, Maputo
Tel (258-1) 49 02 18, 49 02 22/3, 49 04 35
Fax (258-1) 49 14 60

National Information Office,
Av Francisco Orlando Mugwambe, 780, Maputo
Tel (258-1) 49 21 75
Fax (258-1) 49 23 86
Email gabinfo@teledata.cprm.net gabinfo@gabinfo.uem.mz

Bureau of Public Information (BIP),
Av Francisco Orlando Mugwambe, 780, 1st floor, PO Box 2558, Maputo
Tel (258-1) 49 02 00
Fax (258-1) 49 26 22
Email bureaubip@bip.uem.mz

ISBN O-7974-1807-5

Produced by the Southern African Research and Documentation Centre (SARDC) office in Maputo, Mozambique.
Email: sardc@sardcmo.uem.mz
Fax: (258-1) 490831 Tel: (258-1) 491178
Other SARDC offices:
Harare, Zimbabwe
Email: sardc@mango.zw or sardc@samara.co.zw
Fax: (263-4) 738693 Tel. (263-4) 738694/5/6
Dar es Salaam, Tanzania
Fax: (255-51) 110447 Tel.(255-51) 666091/666078

Photographs by David Martin, APG, Harare; Cahora Bassa by Photographic Training Centre, Maputo; S Machel photo from AIM, Maputo; J Chissano photo Fernando Timane, Maputo
Design and Maps by Inkspots Design Studio, Harare, Zimbabwe.
Origination by Crystal Graphics and Printed by Strand Multiprint.

Publication funded by Canadian International Development Agency (CIDA) office in Maputo, Mozambique.

CIDA is providing assistance to Mozambique in the areas of education, health, governance, human rights and democratic development, as well as food supply.